# The River Soar

## IN OLD PHOTOGRAPHS

# The River Soar

## IN OLD PHOTOGRAPHS

Collected by DON WIX,
PAULINE SHACKLOCK *and* IAN KEIL

*Alan Sutton Publishing Limited*
*Phoenix Mill . Far Thrupp*
*Stroud · Gloucestershire*

**ALAN SUTTON**

First Published 1992

Copyright © Don Wix, Pauline Shacklock and
Ian Keil, 1992

**British Library Cataloguing
in Publication Data**

Wix, Don
    River Soar in Old Photographs
    I. Title
    942.54
    ISBN 0-7509-0250-7

Typeset in 9/10 Sabon.
Typesetting and origination by
Alan Sutton Publishing Limited.
Printed in Great Britain by
WBC Print Ltd, Bridgend.

This book is dedicated to the memory of the late
Wallace Humphrey whose love and knowledge
of local history led him to begin the research
with us.

Thirty-seven thousand years ago reindeer wandered above the old river valley, a tundra
landscape fed by melting snow. Antlers and jawbones have been found in the gravels.

# Contents

Fishing the Soar below the ford at Ratcliffe-on-Soar in the 1940s.

# Introduction

The most important river in Leicestershire, the Soar, divides the county into two parts and marks a boundary between the Charnwood Forest heights and the gently rolling undulations of the Wolds. Its broad valley runs from south to north for forty miles and its wide flood plain provides the longest continuous stretch of meadowland in the county. The gravel terraces, significantly above flood level within the broad valley, have provided sites for town and village settlements close to the river. The largest of these settlements are Leicester and Loughborough.

Since the last Ice Age ended about eight thousand years ago the Soar and its tributaries may have served, as W.G. Hoskins suggested, 'as signposts or lifelines into the unknown interior'. Accessible water was a first essential for human life. Although the complete archaeological picture of the Soar in prehistoric times is patchy, evidence shows that successive settlers found the Soar Valley particularly attractive. The Romans founded *Ratae* (now Leicester) at the point where the Fosse Way, joining with the road that ran from Colchester to the Midlands, crossed over the Soar. The town served as capital for the tribe, the *Corieltauvi*.

The name 'Soar' is probably of Romano-British origin and the fact that it remained unchanged implies that successive settlers, notably Anglo-Saxons and, later, Vikings, accepted it and the obvious advantages offered by the river. It had strategic importance, serving as a boundary between settlements and estates. The course of the river north of Loughborough is today the boundary between Nottinghamshire and Leicestershire.

The soils of the valley terraces were fertile and the flood lands provided the meadows which were a vital agricultural resource. These produced the crops of hay that enabled working and breeding livestock to be kept throughout the winter. This remained a valuable agricultural asset even until recent times and rents for meadow land equalled or exceeded rents for the best arable land for centuries.

The Leicestershire Domesday Survey of 1086 showed that the majority of settlements with water-mills were in the Soar Valley. Early pack-horse bridges and fords enabled transport methods to be improved and extended, and the many villages which were bridge settlements became more important.

However, conflict often arose between the many users of the river over whose needs had priority: water for powering mills needed weirs to control flows, but these impeded boats carrying people or goods; fisheries flourished when the water was not polluted with chemicals and waste. Pollution of the river has been a long-term problem. In the seventeenth century the town rules for Quorn forbade the treatment of flax stems in a stream that would be used for drinking water and which eventually fed the Soar. In the later nineteenth century the medical officer of health for the Belgrave Local Health Board, Dr Wilson Emms, complained to the town council of Leicester about allowing untreated sewage into the Soar upstream. This practice endangered the health of people whose drinking water came from the river.

Undoubtedly the industrial expansion of Leicestershire in the later eighteenth century owed much to the creation of the Soar Navigation from the Trent as far as Loughborough. This was achieved by 1779 and its commercial success led to the extension of the canal system to Leicester. The prosperity of the canals declined as the advantages of the railway were realized, but today pleasure cruisers queue at the locks for access to quiet stretches of the river.

The Soar's contributions to economic life during the nineteenth and twentieth centuries are evident from the gasworks and electricity generating stations located on its banks, both needing water and the coal delivered by barges for fuel. Leisure activities have been part of the river scene for centuries; bathing and the enjoyment of the natural history of the waters were succeeded by commercial river trips during the past century. Today leisure interests in the Soar are diverse and include fishing, swimming, boating, rowing, sailing and cruising.

Management of the river to mitigate the damaging effects of floods and the inevitable pollution and yet meet the sometimes conflicting needs of its users is an important and complex task. It involves many landowners, public companies and authorities, and underlies the continuing importance of the Soar.

The complex history of the River Soar has fascinated us. We were obliged to ignore its tributaries because of the vast number of illustrations we found of the Soar itself. We hope that this record will be enjoyed and remind everyone of the riches of our landscape.

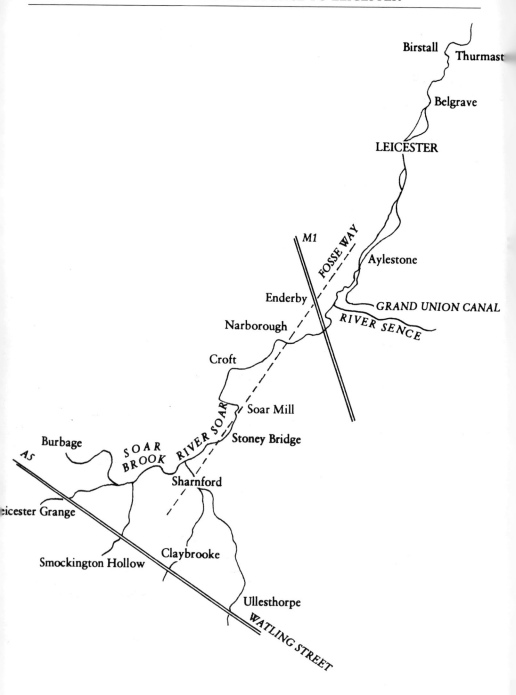

Although parkland is highlighted on this early map of Leicestershire, the River Soar is clearly prominent among the other features. The river divided the county uplands of Charnwood Forest on the west from the rolling hills of the Wolds to the east. During its forty mile course through lush meadows the Soar marked parish boundaries and to the north of Loughborough it became the county boundary of Leicestershire with Nottinghamshire.

# SECTION ONE

# The Source of the Soar

Near to its source at Burbage the Soar is little more than a ditch. Other similar sources are at Leicester Grange, Smockington Hollow, Claybrooke and Ullesthorpe.

The waters of the Soar, even at its source, have been used for work purposes for centuries. Claybrooke Mill stands on one of the streams that forms the source of the river. A water-mill existed on the site by the thirteenth century but the present building dates from the late seventeenth century. The water turned a pitch-back overshot wheel 11 ft in diameter and 5 ft wide. The mechanism was constructed of wood and drove grindstones like those set into the wall.

Douglas Mountford checks the flour produced from the restored mill in recent years.

The old ford at Sharnford, where the Fosse Way crosses the waters. Sharnford is the first town after the point where three streams meet to form the Soar Brook.

Just north of Sharnford by the old Fosse Way the Soar is still little more than a stream. In times of heavy rain, however, it has been known to flood.

The old bridge at Sharnford was built to avoid the hazards of the ford.

An early scene at Watery Lane, Sharnford. The raised foot-bridge to the left and the name of the lane suggest problems in times of flooding.

Stoney Bridge carries the Roman Fosse Way over the Soar not far from a busy modern road. The river has become wider here, joined by another tributary from Claybrooke after leaving Sharnford.

The miller at Soar Mill rows his wife and family on the mill-pond, c. 1898. Soar Mill is the first water-mill on the River Soar proper. The present buildings are largely Victorian with an adjacent Georgian cottage and traces of earlier building. The mill had a breast-shot wheel about 13 ft in diameter. It ceased being a working mill around 1934, since when it has had diverse uses. It underwent a period of sympathetic restoration in the 1970s during which the mill-pond was restored to its original position. Many alterations have been made since it was adapted to its present use as a motel.

The scene above shows the rectory of Croft in 1857. The house was demolished in 1876 and the new rectory built on a different site to the west of the original building (below). The glebe farm was farmed by the rector. At this point the Soar Brook, slightly strengthened by tributaries, is classed as the River Soar for the first time.

The pile of timber by the river at Croft is to be used to build a new bridge in 1857.

Scaffolding surrounds the building of the new bridge at Croft in 1857.

The new bridge at Croft is complete.

Charles H. Robottom invented his own machine for dredging the Soar before 1907. There was a scoop that was filled with mud and then swung back. It was also in the interest of the local rector, the Revd James Brookes, to keep the river dredged because he enjoyed fishing. Every week he put on waders and raked the bottom clean.

Skating was very popular at Croft in 1890. Mr Swain owned a field which bordered the river. He had it flattened and used the spare soil to build a raised bank on three sides of it. On the fourth side was the Soar, bridged at each end of the field. Sluice gates (below), built under the bridges, allowed the field to be flooded to a depth of 1 to 2 ft in mid-winter. During suitably cold weather the water froze and provided safe skating. Sometimes, if the water got low, a fire-engine would pump in more water through a hole in the ice. Tea-rooms alongside the field provided hot refreshments. Special trains brought many skaters from Leicester and at night oil lamps on posts illuminated the scene.

Children fishing for tiddlers in the river at Croft to the left of where the old sheep wash began. A sheep wash usually had to be dug out as it had to be 4 or 5 ft deep in the middle. The sheep were driven in one by one and when they reached the deepest part they were caught by a neck crook and pushed backwards and under the water before they swam out the other side. This was done about ten days before shearing in order to clean the fleece.

In 1932 the severe floods at Croft prompted this boat to be brought in from Huncote to rescue people marooned in their houses by the Soar. The very narrow boat could enter the front door to collect folk inside.

The bridge over the Soar at Narborough before the railway was built in 1864. On the left is the old mill-pond (now gone) and just off the picture would have been the water-mill that had to be demolished to make way for the railway. Upstream lies Narborough bog, an area of 21 acres bounded by the Soar and the M1 where it crosses the Leicester and Birmingham railway line. The bog consists of woodland and reed swamp and contains the largest accumulation of peat in the county, together with an area of marshy meadow to the south. The site, unique in the county, may have been caused by a rise in the water level of the Soar due to the building of weirs. There have been signs of the bog drying out in recent years – again possibly due to control works on the river. The area has been managed by the Leicestershire and Rutland Trust for Nature Conservation since 1975.

Two hump-back bridges at Narborough. The bridge on the left bears an inscription plate to state that it was erected by subscription in 1788. Both have now been demolished.

Enderby Mill was mentioned in 'Domesday Book'. It ceased being a working corn-mill in 1957, having enjoyed a continuous tenancy for nearly nine hundred years. The surviving building dates from the mid-nineteenth century.

This wheel was used at Enderby Mill. The wheel and gears were removed in 1963 when the mill was converted into a pigeon loft.

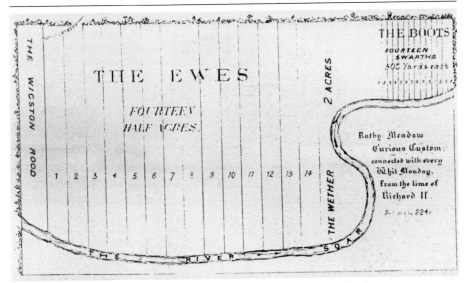

This plan of the meadow by the Soar at Enderby shows divisions named The Ewes, The Boots and The Wether. According to legend, fourteen men were celebrating haymaking when John of Gaunt joined them. He later gave each man half an acre and 300 square yards of meadow, with a plot owned in common, to pay for the haymaking celebrations.

Enderby pack-horse bridge was built in the Middle Ages over the River Soar. Now it stands in splendid isolation as a result of the road being re-routed and, in 1967, the river being diverted to a new course to limit the effects of flooding.

King's Lock is on the Grand Union Canal just before it joins the Soar at Aylestone. It takes its name from George King who was lock-keeper here from 1855 until 1900. He was succeeded by George Swanwick, whose wife and son, Arthur, are walking on the tow-path around 1908. Harrison's Seed Merchants had their trial grounds just south of the lock cottage and Miss Harrison can also be seen on the photograph. Early in the century the boat-house owner installed rollers near King's Lock so that boats could be hauled on to the Blaby stretch of the Soar.

Mr Biggs' boating station off Middleton Street, Aylestone, was a popular rendezvous during the 1920s and 1930s as it lay near to the tram terminus from Leicester. Punts, canoes and rowing-boats were all for hire and attracted many customers on warm summer days. During the First World War soldiers recovering at Leicester Base Hospital were often treated to guided walks by the streams or rowed on the river wearing their bright blue uniforms.

The boating station at Aylestone was located near to the hump-back bridge.

ddleton Street bridge in the 1930s. The bridge was becoming rather narrow for the ving volume of traffic.

The medieval pack-horse bridge at Aylestone. There were niches at various places to allow those on foot to pass larger traffic such as an animal with saddle-bags.

This scene gives an impression of the speed of the locomotives that crossed the Great Central Railway bridge over the Soar at Aylestone. The Great Central line was abandoned after the Beeching Axe curtailed British railways during the mid-1960s.

# Aylestone, Leicester and Belgrave

The castle and St Mary de Castro in the late 1790s. Throsby's view from the canalized River Soar shows a barge being towed by a horse.

Boys fishing by Middleton Street bridge in Aylestone, *c.* 1910. This attractive hump-back bridge had to be pulled down in 1958.

Middleton Street bridge, Aylestone, 1958. The bridge was built in response to the heavier traffic, partly a result of the expansion of Leicester that had absorbed Aylestone, making it a suburb of the city. Vehicle ownership was also increasing, making change essential. The new bridge is named Freestone, commemorating the councillor who instigated the work.

The first gas company in Leicester was established by Act of Parliament in 1821 and it was sited by the canal at Belgrave Gate. A first customer was Leicester Corporation who wanted to illuminate the main streets with gas lights. By 1878 the Corporation became sole owners of the company. The population of Leicester was growing rapidly and increased demand for gas for lighting and for heating made it imperative to expand production. The company also took it upon itself to supply a number of the surrounding villages extending from Birstall to Aylestone and Oadby to New Parks. Aylestone Gasworks was erected, with railway links to the Midland Railway and with the advantages of waterborne supplies of fuel as well as water which proximity to the river offered.

Although Belgrave Gasworks continued to produce gas until 1954, the major developments took place at the Aylestone works of which these retort houses formed a part. Town gas was made at Aylestone until May 1969 when natural gas became the only source of supply. The gasometers remain at Aylestone together with control and maintenance facilities and the John Doran Gas Museum.

Aylestone Electricity Power Station was erected by Leicester Borough Council to supply the needs of the town. The electric tramway service began in 1904 and demand for electricity rose as its versatility as a source of heat, power and light became more widely appreciated. The power station was located next to the gasworks. Coal was supplied either by barge or by railway according to where it came from. The necessity for large supplies of water for use in the cooling towers and the steam generators made the Soar site especially attractive.

Men fishing for coal that had fallen from barges during unloading in 1912. Between February and April that year a national miners' strike caused fuel prices to rise as shortages developed. The wagons belonged to the Midland Railway and were near to the West Bridge terminus of the Leicester and Swannington line.

The weir on the Soar near Aylestone Road in Leicester was one of the ways of keeping water levels under control for navigation.

The River Soar caused flooding in the Saffron Lane area on various occasions. The extent of the flood in the 1970s meant that widespread disruption and problems ensued.

On Whit Tuesday 1866 the Leicester lifeboat was launched at mid-day by St Sunday's Bridge before a crowd of thirty thousand people. The Midland Railway Company carried the boat from the builders to Leicester and afterwards to Gorleston near Great Yarmouth. Four horses hauled the boat on a dray from Campbell Street station to its launch, preceded by the band of the Volunteer Rifles. Sailors manned the boat and demonstrated its self-righting design in the Soar. It had been purchased for the NLI by collections from the working class. Most firms in Leicester gave employees a holiday for the occasion.

A crossing near Frog Island in the 1960s.

Friars Mill is one of the oldest industrial buildings in Leicester. Built in the style of many eighteenth-century factories, the bells at the top of the roof enabled managers to signal the times of shifts to workers, most of whom lived close by. The factory made worsted for the hosiery and knitwear trades of Leicester. The family firm of Donisthorpe owned the factory and joined forces with the Ellises in the second half of the nineteenth century. The firm continues as Donisthorpe, making thread at Friars Mill.

Many firms sought locations by the waterways in central Leicester. Among the developments were factories and warehouses such as the North Mill on Frog Island, shown as it was early in the twentieth century. For much of the nineteenth century the firm of Brewin and Whetstone spun worsted in this factory.

Soldiers load a barge at the Belgrave Ordnance depot during the Second World War.

This privately owned boat was converted by members of the Leicester Fire Brigade for special fire-fighting duties during the Second World War.

A boatman passes reed beds near Leicester Castle in the eighteenth century.

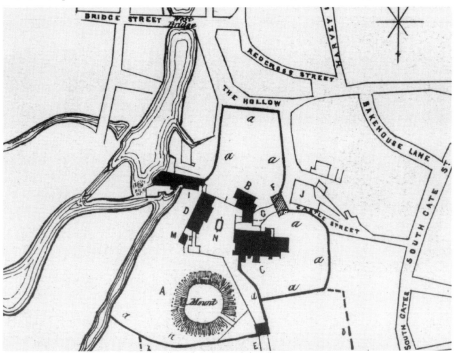

This map of the mid-nineteenth century shows: A, original mound of the Norman castle; B, Castle House; C, St Mary de Castro; D, Castle Hall; E, turret gateway; F, former entry; G, Porter's lodge; H, the magazine; I, Castle Mill; J, gun dykes; K, Prince Rupert's Tower; L, angular tower; M, old dungeon; N, gibbet; a, castle walls; b, Newarke walls.

This prospect of Leicester from the south-east in 1845 shows a train approaching the city. To the right stands the newly built prison with its castellated brick walls on the Welford Road. This was then on the outskirts. The many factory chimneys indicate the importance of coal as a source of energy. Much coal still came in barges along the Soar and the clustering of the factories marks the course of the river and its cuts.

Leicester city councillors were inspecting river conditions in 1973 with the intention of improving the Soar as an amenity for the city. The *Erewash Princess* was passing the home of the sea cadets at Ross Walk.

A horse and cart has just crossed the Newarke or Drayton Bridge in 1918. This was one of Leicester's newer bridges, opened in 1902. Previously there was a wooden foot-bridge here leading to the old vicarage.

Bow Bridge took its name from the narrow foot-bridge that stood only a few yards away to the north-west and had a single arch in the shape of a bow. It was built for the Austin Friars who used it to fetch water from St Austin's well. This was a pure spring that was covered by a large stone with a hole in the centre through which the friars could lower and fill their vessels.

The medieval Bow Bridge or King Richard's Bridge was rebuilt in 1666. It had five low arches with low parapet walls and there were niches at either side where pedestrians could stand when traffic was passing. It lay close to the West Bridge and Richard III rode over it at the head of his cavalry on his way to Bosworth Field in 1485, his corpse returning the same way after the battle. He was buried in the Grey Friar's church of St Mary de Pre, but after the Dissolution of the Monasteries his body was disinterred and cast into the river by Bow Bridge.

Bow Bridge is shown just before it was taken down in 1861. It had been in a very dilapidated state for some years and there was a need to replace it with a wider one.

The West Bridge was one of the oldest entrances to Leicester and was built early in the twelfth century. It spanned the River Soar just beyond the West Gate until 1774. In 1325 the bridge was reconstructed in stone and timber, and restored again in 1365. During the fourteenth century a chapel was built over its eastern end. This was dedicated to Our Lady of the Bridge and belonged to the College of St Mary de Castro. It was customary for any visiting royalty or important person to be met by the Corporation at the West Bridge. When the bridge was demolished in 1841 the chapel served as a barber's shop.

Near the West Bridge the 'ducking stool' was used for punishing 'scolds' of the town in the sixteenth century. This was a barbaric method of dealing with women who voiced their complaints too loudly and for too long. They were tied to the stool that hung from a pivoted pole over the river and plunged into the water as many times as their misdemeanour had been judged to warrant. Unfortunately many were almost drowned in the process.

A new West Bridge was built in 1842 by the Corporation. This was a wider iron bridge of a single arch and cost £4,000. To the north was a coal wharf at the terminus of the Leicester and Swannington Railway that had been built in 1833 from the coalfield to Leicester. From this wharf coal was carried by barge along the canal.

Increasing traffic and the need for a still wider bridge led to a further West Bridge being built in 1891. At this time the river was widened under Leicester Corporation's Flood Relief Scheme and a temporary wooden bridge was built alongside while the permanent bridge was completed.

The West Bridge on completion was a handsome structure. In 1784 thousands of spectators assembled here and upon the bank when the Soar became so frozen that a masquerade was held upon it near Vauxhall Gardens. Harlequin, Columbine, Pantaloon and the Clown were represented.

A little to the south of the North Bridge lay another medieval bridge, Frogmire, or Little North Bridge, that is likely to have originally been a wooden one. It crossed a small arm of the River Soar and the 'island' between the two bridges has retained the name Frog Island. With the advent of the navigation the bridge in Northgate became a cast-iron 'canal' bridge constructed to carry heavy traffic.

The Great Central Railway line passed through the middle of Leicester and crossed the Soar or its cuts six times. The canal at Frog Island was one of the places where the viaduct could be seen under construction during the 1890s.

The North or St Sunday's Bridge is known to have existed in 1365 and formed the northern entrance to the town crossing the main stream of the River Soar outside the North Gate. It was given the name St Dominic by the Dominican Order of Preaching Friars who were housed near the North Bridge, the English equivalent of the name being St Sunday. The old North Bridge was of stone with ten arches and was 98 yd and 1 ft long. It was washed away by a severe flood in 1795 and a new three-arched bridge replaced it as shown. This, in turn, was rebuilt in 1867–8 as an iron girder bridge to carry heavy traffic. The tramway from the town to Groby Road passed over it.

The medieval stone bridge at Belgrave is known to have existed in 1357. It originally linked the two parts of Belgrave parish and lay on the great highway from London, Leicester, Manchester and Carlisle. It consisted of seven arches, the arch nearest the tow-path being rebuilt in 1793 to enable canal boats to pass after the river had been canalized. On the south side of the bridge was the site of Belgrave Wharf, at one time a busy site for the unloading of Mountsorrel granite used in road making.

Thurmaston Road bridge in Leicester was replaced shortly after this photograph was taken in 1916. Preparations for the new crossing were under way at the time.

The public wharf at Belgrave Gate, Leicester, in the 1890s was used for transhipments. Casks frequently contained a wide variety of products apart from liquids. The smoke rising from the chimney on one of the barges reminds us that many bargees lived on their craft with their families.

The elderly lady steering the barge at the beginning of the twentieth century reminds us of the hard physical tasks that men and women endured in those days.

The wharf at Belgrave Road, Leicester, 1956. Coils of steel strip are being loaded on to barges that would take them to London docks where they would be stowed in ships for a Spanish customer. British Waterways began to trade as a nationalized company in 1948.

## FLY BOATS.

*From Deacon, Harrison, and Co.'s Wharf, Navigation-street.*

To LONDON—every Wednesday, Friday, and Saturday evening, in 60 hours.

*From Shenton's Wharf, Navigation-street.*

To SHARDLOW—every Tuesday and Saturday evening; from which place goods are forwarded by *Messrs. Soresby and Flack* to Derby, the Staffordshire Potteries, Manchester, and Liverpool: also to Birmingham, Stourport, Bristol, Bridgewater, and all parts of the West of England.

*From Pickford and Co.'s Wharf, West Bridge.*

To LONDON, Oxford, Baubury, Northampton, and all parts of the South—every Tuesday, Thursday, Friday, and Saturday

To LIVERPOOL, Manchester, Birmingham, Bristol, Worcester, Derby, and all parts of the North and West—every Tuesday, Thursday, Friday, and Saturday.

To NOTTINGHAM—every Tuesday and Friday.

*From Ella, Coleman, and Co. Wharfingers.*

To all Parts of England—daily.

The (Old) Grand Union Canal Company absorbed the canalized Soar in 1810. In due course this formed part of the canal network that linked the Midlands with London. The extent of the business by 1828 is illustrated by the advertisement taken from the Leicestershire County Directory.

The rates of tonnage, according to the act, from Loughborough to Leicester, are—

|  |  |  |
|---|---|---|
| For coals | - | 1s. 2d. per ton. |
| Iron, timber, &c. | | 2s. 6d. |

Quantity of the articles brought by this canal:

|  | *tons.* |
|---|---|
| Coal annually consumed in Leicester and its vicinity | 35,000 |
| Ditto forwarded to other canals | 18,000 |
| Merchandize for Leicester | 4,000 |
| Ditto sent down (chiefly wool) | 1,600 |

The cost of canal transport in the 1820s was also illustrated in the 1828 directory. The volume of traffic mentioned allowed the town of Leicester to expand its manufactures to support its growing population.

The Abbey Meadows, at Leicester; an illustration from John Nichol's *History of Leicestershire* written at the end of the eighteenth century. The Earl of Leicester founded the Augustinian Abbey of St Mary in 1143. It became the second wealthiest house in the Order in England before it was dissolved as a consequence of the Reformation in 1538.

The Abbey ruins in tranquil parkland by the River Soar in the early twentieth century. The Abbey was the final destination of Cardinal Wolsey who died there in 1530. He was, by then, in disgrace and likely to have faced unpleasant treatment from King Henry VIII.

A crew row past Abbey Park during the 1930s.

Various facilities were erected in Abbey Park during the years after the First World War. One was the house in the background which was used for meetings and as a restaurant and café for people enjoying a visit.

The August Bank Holiday Show was held in Abbey Park in 1905. Various competitions were held on the Monday and the Tuesday. One event was the swimming gala at which, in 1905, B.B. Kieran won the English half-mile championship. There was a bathing station at Abbey Meadows a short distance downstream where competitive events were held in the 1890s and in the early years of the twentieth century.

The crowd endured a wet summer day in Abbey Park soon after the public park opened. The foot-bridge over the River Soar was one of the attractions.

# ABBEY PARK

## LEICESTER.

### TUESDAY, AUGUST 2nd, 1887,

# GRAND FLOWER SHOW & GALA

REGATTA AND WATER SPORTS.
MILITARY AND OTHER BANDS. GRAND
BALLOON ASCENTS. DANCING, &c.

For further particulars see small bills.

Secretary and Curator, Mr. JOHN BURN.

# LEICESTER ROWING CLUB.

# REGATTA,

### TUESDAY, August 2nd, 1887,

### ABBEY PARK,

### RACES for Fours, Pairs, Sculls.

# WATER SPORTS,

UPSET CANOE RACE.   AQUATIC DERBY
SWIMMING.

Commence at Twelve o'clock.

Leicester Rowing Club's annual regatta was held as part of Abbey Park Flower Show and Gala in the late 1880s. The president held 'a large garden party on the pleasant banks of the river with his usual hospitality'. Pair oars and sculling races were over half a mile while fours races were over one mile. Cups and tankards were later filled with champagne.

Rowing is one of Leicester's oldest sports. Leicester Rowing Club was founded in 1882 at Belgrave where the canal stretch was used. As the club grew, Hawleys Dyeworks on Frog Island permitted the building of a boat-house on its land in 1887. Later the club moved to an allotment garden site near to Abbey Gate. The river course in that area was nearly a mile long and there were twenty boats. In 1906 another boat-house was built at the bottom of Filbert Street. It housed 6 fours, 4 pairs, 3 whiffs, and 8 tubs on the ground floor. Upstairs were dressing-rooms and showers. When Leicester Power Station was constructed the club moved across the canal to its present site.

The Leicester Regatta of 1887 attracted many spectators to its various events.

The engraving of Belgrave Mill shows the water-wheel powered by water from the River Soar. This mill stood between Belgrave Hall and Belgrave Lock. In the twentieth century sea cadets trained on *TS Tiger* on the site of the mill.

The grounds of Belgrave Hall extend to the River Soar. The hall was built by Edmund Cradock of Knighton Hall near Leicester and was completed in 1715. The Vann family lived in the house for about a century before it passed into the hands of John Ellis who became chairman of the Midland Railway Company in 1849. It is now a museum run by Leicestershire County Council.

A toll-house was built by the new bridge at Belgrave in 1835. In about 1830 plans were made to straighten the road from the town to the foot of Birstall Hill. A bridge was therefore built with five arches, the middle arch being large enough to take the river traffic. The total cost was £6,500. Tolls were collected at both Belgrave old and Belgrave new gates until the termination of the turnpike trust in the 1870s. In 1836 a record amount of £6,800 was taken from traffic using the Loughborough to Harborough Road, representing 350,000 horses. This can be compared with 1726 when tolls were first collected – £400 representing 90,000 horses.

This artistic creation of the lock house by Michael Barker is based on the memories of Mr Harry Godfrey who lived there from 1926.

A horse-drawn barge passes Belgrave on its way along the canalized Soar to Leicester.

People enjoying pleasure-boating near Belgrave during the Edwardian era.

The old Belgrave boat-house was sold in 1965 to Leicester Youth Service as an outdoor pursuits centre. The activities of canoeing and canoe-building were then extended to include many other challenging pastimes.

In the 1920s these covered motor boats belonging to Noakes and Co. were based near Belgrave boat-house and made trips from Loughborough Road bridge in Leicester every Thursday, Saturday and Sunday through the summer. Costs of return trips were: Cossington Mill, 2s 6d; Mountsorrel, 3s 5d; Loughborough, 4s 6d; Normanton-on-Soar, 5s 6d. Catering could be arranged.

The Soar overflowed its banks early in the twentieth century to make the streets of Belgrave difficult, but not impassable.

The sewage works, built by Leicester Corporation, pumped waste liquids to a treatment plant at Beaumont Leys. Erected at the end of the nineteenth century, these works were superseded after the Second World War and became the home of the Museum of Technology.

# SECTION THREE

# Birstall, Thurmaston, Wanlip and Cossington

A quiet stretch of water in the area of Birstall.

In 1086 the Domesday Survey reported two mills in the Birstall and Thurmaston area. In 1751 Birstall Mill was a water-mill used to grind corn; The miller was Thomas Saunders and the population of Birstall was around 250 people. The chimney was a later addition. In around 1820 John Mansfield MP restored the mill, together with other buildings in the village, to working order. In 1903 it became a leather board mill.

Birstall Wharf by Whitehorse Lane was once a busy site. The White Horse Inn served the canal folk. Coal was unloaded from the barges and wheeled to the inn yard. The landlords were usually coal merchants as well. The small bridge to the right spanned the mill stream.

The locals at Birstall watch with interest as men repair and clean out the lock just after the Second World War.

Birstall Lock affords a rise of just over three feet.

It appears that Birstall in 1969 is suddenly a seaside resort. The truth is that the main river course borders the housing estate while the rest is flooded meadowland.

Rowing-boats take a peaceful outing between Birstall and Belgrave, *c.* 1910.

The 'one-armed' bridge by Birstall weir has a wintry look earlier in the century. Since then it has been rebuilt with concrete as the main building material.

An old view of the tow-path at Birstall shows a backwater to the right. The canal winds under the bridge and the mill stream is out of sight to the left.

North of Birstall the river is shallow and the common reed (*Phragmites australis*) grows in the margins providing good nesting sites for reed warblers. There are reed beds in a number of places along the Soar and for centuries the reeds were harvested and used for thatching.

Thurmaston Mill was mentioned in 'Domesday Book' and was working until the 1920s. In 1860 it was bought from its owner by the Leicester Navigation Company, it being the policy of the canal company to acquire water-mills, if possible, in order to control the water rights. This mill was destroyed by fire before 1930. At that time it had been partly in use as a tea-room. The site has been used since as a boat-yard.

A pleasure-boat bringing children and teachers of Thurmaston Primitive Methodist Sunday School under Johnson's Bridge, 1909. This was the Sunday school's annual treat, and no doubt they would have disembarked at a suitable place for some games and a good tea before returning home.

These skaters on the frozen river at Thurmaston are making the most of a long period of freezing weather in the early years of the twentieth century. There were various recognized places along the river and canal where skaters were quick to enjoy their sport, should weather conditions be suitable.

Thurmaston village, seen from across the water, was a busy place when the navigation was at its prime. There were three wharves here where coal and other commodities were unloaded before being taken further afield by horse and cart. There is a weir by Johnson's Bridge at the north end of the village, which where the River Soar links up with the canal.

These were the last two working boats in the county. They were owned by Three Fellowes Carrying Company and plied to and fro taking unwashed gravel from pits near Birstall to Wanlip, where it was washed and graded. They ceased working as late as 1989–90.

This peaceful stretch of the Soar flowing by Wanlip was left untouched by the navigation. This was due to the action of Mr Grave Hudson who, in the 1790s, managed to have a clause inserted into the Act of Parliament which permitted the canal to be built. The clause forbade the proprietors from building the canal within sight of Wanlip Hall. For this reason a section of canal leaves the north end of Thurmaston and curves round to join the River Wreake, that is itself canalized for one mile before linking with the Soar south of Cossington Mill.

Built for a less mobile age, this hump-back bridge over the Soar at Wanlip in 1967 was soon to be replaced by a modern bridge built to carry heavy road traffic.

The Hope and Anchor on the canal at Wanlip was described as an inn in 1846 and, like many of these businesses, had facilities for stabling the horses that pulled the narrow boats. There was also a coal wharf here to serve the local village. The building and its surroundings have been modernized and altered a great deal over the years.

Wanlip sewage treatment works was opened in November 1964 with equipment enabling it to meet the increasing demand from Leicester. After processing, water present in the sewage was clean enough to pass into the Soar. For some years the works sold a garden fertilizer known as Lescost.

The River Soar and the canalized River Wreake meet approximately 100 yd south of Cossington Mill. Then almost immediately they divide into a weir and a navigable lock. The water from the high level was led by a mill-race to the mill-wheel. Afterwards the water flowed into the mill-pond.

The old foot-bridge that crossed the River Soar at the back of Cossington Mill had become very dilapidated and unsafe by the 1950s. Shortly afterwards it was replaced by the more substantial structure shown below.

The site of Cossington Mill is first mentioned in 1248. The present mill buildings date from the early seventeenth century. In 1477 it was described as a corn- and fulling-mill, but by 1651 it was a corn-mill only. In 1657 it became a corn- and paper-mill, but reverted to a corn-mill again in the middle of the nineteenth century. The last miller, Henry Gardner, left in 1928. The undershot wheel was housed in a small wheel-house between the mill and the mill house. The machinery was removed when the mill closed. The mill buildings have often been isolated by flooding throughout their history.

The mill house was erected in the early nineteenth century and has for many years supported a magnificent wisteria.

The old hump-back bridge next to Cossington Lock was an attractive scene beloved of artists and photographers alike. It posed a serious problem when traffic increased along the Rothley to Cossington road. Weight restrictions were placed on the bridge but the growth of traffic was such that it ultimately had to be replaced by a stronger bridge.

A motor launch has just come through Cossington Lock. Some idea of the pollution in the 1950s can be gained from the foam surrounding the boat and on the sides of the lock.

The footpath across the fields from Cossington to Sileby Mill has been flooded innumerable times.

A line of traffic going through the floods was a fairly common sight until the road from Cossington to Rothley was raised and realigned.

This stretch of river to the north of Cossington Mill has become popular during the twentieth century for sailing. All kinds of pleasure-craft are used here.

Boys on the landing-stage at Ratcliffe College Boat Club. In 1939 permission was given to house boats at Cossington Mill and with a gift of two shell fours and a tub pair named *Teach-me* the club was born. Later a strip of land was purchased opposite Cossington Bridge and a boat-house was built in 1940 for £500. Soon two skiffs and two canoes were purchased. In 1946 three secondhand clinker fours were added to the fleet and were named *Terence* and *Baillons* after old boys killed in the war. In the October gales of 1987 the boat-house blew down and was re-erected by staff.

As more new boats were purchased by Ratcliffe College the older ones were stored under the boat-house. By 1969 the college could boat up to seven crews at any one time. Eights were never used because the cornering at speed round the right-angle Soar bends would be dangerous. In 1969 a 42 ft catamaran named *Peter and Paul*, constructed at the college, was ceremoniously launched. It seated four oarsmen at each side with a platform down the centre for coaching. With four new boats, in the 1970s and 1980s, the college was well able to train for competition. In recent times, with more sporting activities on offer and other changes within the college, fewer students are rowing but the club remains.

# Sileby, Mountsorrel, Barrow-upon-Soar and Quorn

Sailing is enjoyed on a summer's day between Sileby and Mountsorrel, while swans are always ready to be fed on the river bank. Castle Hill, Mountsorrel, is in the background with its granite war memorial on the top.

Two mills were recorded in 'Domesday Book' at Sileby and it is likely that the present mill stands on one of the original sites. It was a working corn-mill until the end of the nineteenth century, with the miller's cottage adjacent, as shown above, and was one of only two mills in the county using one wheel and two sets of grindstones. The present mill building dates from the eighteenth century, a number of additions being made in the nineteenth and twentieth centuries including the boiler-house chimney.

After ceasing work as a corn-mill the building was used as a leather board mill until 1936. Cardboard waste was pulped in big vats and pressed before being rolled into quarter-inch thick sheets. These were used to make insoles for the shoe trade, Sileby being a flourishing centre for the latter industry. The mill is now a busy marina catering for the needs of the leisure boating world.

The double-arched foot-bridge over the weir at Sileby was rebuilt in 1985.

This race at Sileby brought water from the Soar to drive the mill-wheel.

From the air Sileby Mill can be seen by the side of the navigable canal, with the River Soar meandering through the fields beyond.

The canal lock and basin lie alongside Sileby Mill, the scene of much activity in the era of working boats.

The Waterside Inn at Mountsorrel in 1965. The old lock cottage that had served as a toll-office can be seen in the foreground. It was demolished in 1967. The boat-yard and marina occupy the middle distance.

The marina at Mountsorrel, where a boat hire business, begun in the mid-1960s, has seen busy times.

In 1948 Eric Boon bought a wood yard by the side of the river, next to the canal and started a business building, repairing and selling boats. It was the only firm of its kind between Trent Lock and Leicester at the time. In 1957 he bought three lifeboats from the troopship *Empire Ken* to convert into cabin cruisers. These had both marine engines and sails. They were brought by lorry to Loughborough and then hoisted by crane into the canal before being brought to Mountsorrel.

The Waterside Inn (formerly called The Duke of York) surrounded by floods in 1969. The restaurant was originally stables for the horses that pulled narrow boats on the canal.

A barge on its way through Mountsorrel Lock in 1900. There were two canal wharves at Mountsorrel where coal was brought by barge and unloaded for distribution in neighbouring villages.

The canal joins the Soar at this point near Mountsorrel. Some of the craft shown here, around 1900, have certainly passed their working days.

The tow-path at Mountsorrel has always been a popular walk in the summer months.

Mountsorrel Mill was built in 1775 on Main Street and extended to the river. It was driven by two undershot water-wheels and used to grind corn for local farmers and to supply flour and meal to local bakeries. Mr J.C. Smith owned the mill in the 1870s and worked it until 1912. Various businesses made use of the buildings after they ceased working. For some years it was a leather board mill. The site was cleared in 1960 and a new building and slipway to the river constructed. This then became known as the Marine Centre and catered for the needs of leisure craft.

Granite from Mountsorrel quarries was transported over long distances by water. There was a direct railway link to the navigation from the workings. The remains of two tipplers can be seen where granite was loaded into barges. In 1860 a new mineral line was constructed from the quarry to the Midland Railway Company's main line. It crossed the canal by the brick-built single arch bridge. After its completion most granite was conveyed by rail.

By the early 1970s the osier beds at Mountsorrel show little of their former industrial importance. Osiers were extensively grown all along the river. The species of willow generally planted were *Salix viminalis*, the common osier, and *Salix triandra*, the almond willow. The common sallow, *Salix atrocinerea*, was also used. The beds were planted with 'sets' less than 2 ft apart, from which long straight shoots grew. They were hoed in summer to keep them free of weeds and then cut almost to the ground in winter. Women prepared the harvested crop for market, usually removing the bark. Prepared osiers were used in basket-making, a craft carried on in many villages along the Soar Valley.

Mute swans congregate in great numbers on the river near Sileby Mill and Barrow-upon-Soar.

The Navigation Inn at Barrow-upon-Soar is a familiar landmark to all boating enthusiasts and was built at the same time as the navigation around 1794. For many years it sold ales and stout brewed by Sharpe's of Sileby and it provided stabling for horses that hauled canal barges.

During the night of 22/23 March 1971 the bridge and weir near Barrow-upon-Soar separating the river from the Grand Union Canal collapsed, causing the canal to drain and empty and leaving many boats marooned. The weir was later reconstructed but the bridge was never replaced.

Young boys idling and fishing by the weir in Barrow-upon-Soar, c. 1908. To the right was a further bridge of three arches over a wider stretch of the weir. The whole bridge structure and weir collapsed on the fateful night.

This is the new weir that was built to replace the one washed away in 1971.

'Domesday Book' of 1086 mentioned three mills in the parish of Barrow-upon-Soar. This mill probably stands on the site of one of them. It was owned by the lord of the manor who obliged all villagers to have their corn ground here and to pay a small amount of flour for the service. In 1824 the mill was bought by the Leicester Navigation Company and it ceased to be a corn-mill in 1880 when it was purchased by Mr C. Goodacre for processing gypsum. Gypsum was mined at Kingston-on-Soar and taken to a wharf near Kegworth where it was loaded onto horse-drawn barges before being taken to either the mill at Zouch or on to Barrow for processing into plaster.

Barrow Mill was powered by two large wheels 15 and 20 ft in diameter.

The horse-drawn narrow boat *Kingswood* was owned by Fellows, Morton and Clayton. It is being raised in Barrow deep lock in about 1905 before continuing its way south.

The three-arched bridge at Barrow-upon-Soar was rebuilt in 1845 of local Mountsorrel granite. It replaced an earlier, narrower bridge that stood further upstream.

The tea-room, now the Riverside Restaurant, had been gaily decorated for the coronation of King George V in 1911.

There is an attractive stretch of the river both sides of Barrow Bridge and hiring a rowing-boat has always been a popular pastime.

This sailing-boat was one of a county 'pool' of boats used from the early 1960s to provide sailing lessons for schools. Older pupils from Garendon School, Loughborough, had built the boat and thus contributed to the expansion of water sports – part of the county's out-door pursuits policy.

In the 1970s and '80s a new road was planned to bypass Quorn, Mountsorrel and Rothley. The 'Blue Route', i.e. the river valley route, was selected in preference to the 'Green Route' that would have passed over higher land towards the edge of Charnwood Forest. Choosing the valley route meant that the winding River Soar had to be bridged four times. Huge quantities of local stone were used to embank the road above the flood plain and culverts were constructed to allow the flow of flood water freely across it. Here a bridge is in the course of construction across the river.

These young men are standing by the flooded 'slabs' footpath that crossed the meadow known as Scotch Green from Barrow Bridge to Quorn. Originally the path followed the line of the river as far as Quorn but it was diverted in 1788 when Quorn Hall was occupied by Hugo Meynell, so that it did not pass close by the front of his residence. The path was improved by Mr K. Warner in around 1886 when it was altered to its present course.

Traffic passing through the floods between Barrow and Quorn in the 1930s. This road has always been one of the first to flood in the Soar Valley, but the raised foot-bridge allowed pedestrians to reach their destination safely.

Extensive flooding beside the Soar at Barrow-upon-Soar has challenged water engineers to find ways of controlling abnormal flows.

The tow-path between Barrow Bridge and Pilling's Lock has always attracted anglers and walkers. This area is rich in bird life and flora; 180 different species of flora have been counted between the bridge and the lock, including branched bur-reed, unbranched bur-reed, sweet flag, meadow cranesbill, meadow rue, and teasels. The latter attract gold-finches. Near the lock are good colonies of woundwort.

Pilling's Lock (Barrow Shallow Lock) is so named after a nineteenth-century lock-keeper and it is usually found with both sets of gates open. The lock is necessary, however, when flooding is imminent. The lock-keeper's cottage was pulled down in 1957.

There seemed to be no need for this notice in view of the conditions near Barrow-upon-Soar at the time.

The River Soar adds to this idyllic scene near Barrow-upon-Soar during the 1960s.

The Barrow-upon-Soar limestone quarried for centuries from the lower lias beds have provided lime that was transported by barge away from the area. Limestone from here was used to build the West Bridge in Leicester in 1325, as well as for Leicester Guildhall. These limestones were formed in seas in prehistoric times and have revealed large fossil skeletons of the Ichthyosaur. A special find was the 20 ft long Pleisiosaurus whose skeleton is in Leicestershire Museum and whose shape directs the traffic round Barrow road island.

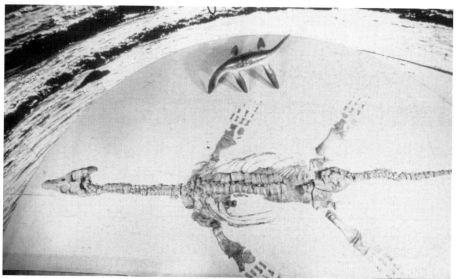

The old limestone workings in Barrow-upon-Soar in 1901 show the folded rocks or anti-clines (above) and more horizontal strata (below).

Quarrymen stand in the limestone workings at Barrow-upon-Soar at the end of the last century. Local limestone was not much used after 1910.

A 200-million-year-old crustacean fossil, *Eryon Barroviensis* (Barrow).

A 'rayfinned' fish fossil, *Heterolepidotus*, which is 200 million years old.

Beadles Pit, near to the Soar at Thurmaston, was once a gravel pit and is now built over. It is an example of the many gravel extraction areas along the Soar Valley floor where sand and gravel have been quarried since the 1850s. Thirty-seven thousand years ago reindeer, mammoth and woolly rhinoceros roamed in a cold tundra landscape. The Soar, fed by melting snows, spread gravel over a wide area. Today the deposits are up to 100 ft thick.

The mammoths of thirty-seven thousand years ago weighed 5 tons, were covered in dark hair, were vegetarian, and lived for fifty or sixty years. Today their tusks (some as long as 12 ft) and teeth are discovered in the gravel deposits during the quarrying process.

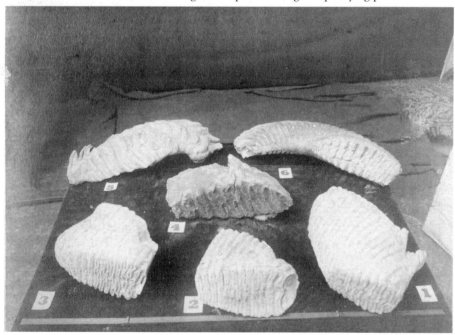

The remains of a woolly rhinoceros being unearthed from gravel at Quorn, 1938.

John Throsby drew Quorndon Hall in 1791. He commented: 'The grand representation in the background of this view is well known in Leicestershire; the forest hills are resting behind Buddon Wood. From Barrow cliff where I took this view the Soar is seen sweetly serpentining and the bridge over it serves as an excellent break in the middle of the view.'

Quorn has always suffered from severe flooding of both the River Soar and Quorn Brook and this has caused much disruption to the lives of the inhabitants. One of the worst floods in living memory was in 1932 and the extent of it can be seen along Leicester Road near to the junction with School Lane.

Some of the youngsters of Quorn play on the flood-boards in School Lane, c. 1904. There were flood-boards on either side of the road near the little bridge to enable children to reach the village school when Quorn Brook was in flood.

Flooding in Soar Road by the side of the river, 1904. The front doors of the cottages to the left were built above street level as a flood precaution and when Wharf House was rebuilt in 1897–8 the new floor was put seven inches above the old flood mark. However, the water rose even above this on New Year's Eve in 1900.

Little girls lean over to pick wild flowers by the side of the river in 1904.

Young men of Quorn seize the opportunity to swim in the river on a warm summer's day, *c.* 1900. There were, conventionally, places where nude bathing took place. A gravestone in All Saints churchyard, Loughborough, records the death of three young men drowned in the River Soar in 1767. It seems that two swimmers got into difficulties and the other died endeavouring to save them. Only one body was clothed.

The gasworks was built in 1853 at the Brinks beside the Soar by Quorn Gas Company at a cost of £3,300. The works converted coal into town gas brought to the site by barge from East Midlands mines. The company supplied Quorn and Mountsorrel. In 1862 Barrow-upon-Soar was connected to the works that were demolished in 1966.

The Soar Brook enters the river near to the Brinks at Quorn.

This cast-iron bridge was built to carry the Midland Counties Railway between Barrow-upon-Soar and Loughborough across the Soar close to the junction of the Grand Union Canal navigation with the river. The bridge was built in 1839 and was later replaced when cast iron ceased to be regarded as suitable for railway bridges.

The circular loop of the Soar that stretches from Barrow to Quorn and back to Barrow is navigable for only about three-quarters of a mile. It is little used so the reach is rich in bird life. Water-birds nest among the reeds and can be seen with their young in spring. The kingfisher (1) still manages to breed on stretches of the river where the bank is vertical. Other birds shown are mallard (2), moorhen (3), and little grebe (4).

# SECTION FIVE

# Loughborough, Cotes and Stanford-on-Soar

The entrance to the Brush Falcon Works at Loughborough is covered with flood waters as this coach leaves the factory before the First World War.

The River Soar in the foreground passes through meadow and pasture lands often flooded during periods of heavy rains in past centuries. The development of Loughborough stopped on the edge of the flood plain. The Midland Railway line skirts the extreme eastern edge of the town separating the Brush engineering works from the town. Running parallel with the top of the photograph, taken in 1953, is the Great Central Railway, that once formed part of the British railway system.

The Soar overflowed its banks frequently and in 1890 the tracks at the Midland Railway station were awash.

The flood waters along the Nottingham Road not only made life difficult at the Midland Railway station, but the waters stretched as far as the approach to the bridge that carried the road over the canal.

The Railway Inn has a make-shift entrance to clear the waters of the flooded Soar early in the twentieth century.

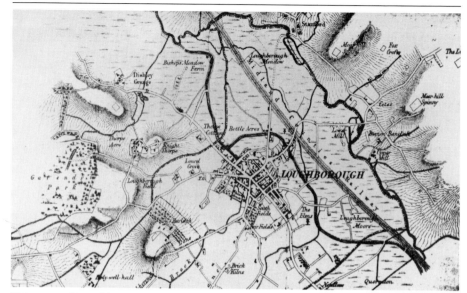

This map of Loughborough dates from the middle of the nineteenth century. It shows the town sited above the flood plain of the River Soar with the canal running into it from the north across Bishop Meadow, and the newer canal built to the east and south for carrying barges to Leicester. The Midland Counties Railway opened in 1840 to link Leicester, Nottingham and Derby. The company joined with the North Midland to form the Midland Railway Company in 1844.

The flat Loughborough Meadows is an important example of the Soar Valley's ability to retain the flora and fauna of the past. There are 178 species of flora here and the long grass gives cover for the breeding whinchats and redshanks.

# LOUGHBOROUGH BIG MEADOW AND DISTRICT.

## GARTON and WOOLLEY

WILL hold their 42ND ANNUAL SALE of MOWING GRASS.

On MONDAY NEXT, JUNE 22nd, including 63 ACRES, as follows:

### BIG MEADOW, LOUGHBOROUGH.

|  | A. | R. | P. |
|---|---|---|---|
| Ed. Hands, Esq. ... ... ... ... ... ... ... | 3 | 1 | 25 |
| Alan Moss, Esq. ... ... ... ... ... ... ... | 8 | 0 | 0 |
| Mr. R. Birkin ... ... ... ... ... ... ... | 4 | 0 | 0 |
| Mr. J. Cartwright ... ... ... ... ... ... | 7 | 2 | 0 |
| Messrs. The Brush Electrical Eng. Co., Ltd. ... ... ... ... ... ... ... | 4 | 0 | 0 |
| Do., do. (near Falcon Works) ... ... ... | 1 | 2 | 0 |
| Mr. J. Hubbard ... ... ... ... ... ... | 3 | 2 | 0 |
| The Trustees of the late Mr. G. Dickens | 7 | 3 | 0 |
| Do. Do. ... ... ... ... ... | 4 | 0 | 0 |
| Mr. P. Moss ... ... ... ... ... ... ... | 7 | 2 | 0 |

### ALLSOPPS LANE, LOUGHBOROUGH.

|  | A. | R. | P. |
|---|---|---|---|
| The Loughborough College (with aftermath) ... ... ... ... ... | 7 | 2 | 0 |

### FOREST ROAD, LOUGHBOROUGH.

|  | A. | R. | P. |
|---|---|---|---|
| Mrs. Underwood, Field along road side | 3 | 2 | 0 |

Please meet at BIG MEADOW GATE, at 6-30 P.M. SHARP; at ALLSOPP'S LANE at 8 P.M.; and at FOREST ROAD at 8-30 P.M.

Auctioneers' Offices: Cattle Market, Loughborough (Tel. 141).

In the 1920s the *Loughborough Echo* advertises the 'Annual Sale of Mowing Grass' on the meadowlands by the Soar. The rich grasses were sold to local farmers to cut as winter feed for their livestock. This very flat land, enriched for thousands of years by silt from the annual floods, has always been unsuitable for building or arable farming purposes.

The Peter Le Marchant Trust was formed in 1975 as a result of a bequest to Clare Hanmer from her brother Peter Le Marchant. The aim was to offer seriously ill and handicapped folk a day out or holiday on the river. The first boat took twelve people for trips. Today there are two well-equipped broad beam boats, *Symphony* and *Serenade*, based at Loughborough and taking up to nine thousand people a year: up to 28 at a time for day trips and 14 for holiday trips. A holiday or even just a day spent travelling slowly along the Soar with its beautiful surroundings continues to give immeasurable pleasure to people of all ages. The top picture shows the early boats on the Kegworth stretch and the lower one the more recent well-appointed broad beam boats.

# A N

# A     C     T

## F O R

*Making the River* Soar *navigable from the River* Trent *to or near* Loughborough, *in the County of* Leicefter; *and for making navigable Cuts or Canals from the faid River* Soar *to or near the* Rufhes *and the* Hermitage Pool *at* Loughborough *aforefaid.*

ᵂᴴᴱᴿᴱᴬᔆ the River *Soar* dividing the Counties Preamble. of *Leicefter* and *Nottingham*, is capable of being made navigable from the River *Trent*, where the faid River *Soar* now falls into the faid River *Trent*, to a certain Place in the Lordfhip of *Loughborough*, in the faid County of *Leicefter*, where a certain Brook, called the *Hermitage Brook*, falls into the faid River *Soar*.

ᴬⁿᵈ ʷʰᵉʳᵉᵃˢ a navigable Cut or Canal may be made from the faid River *Soar*, at or near a Place where the Lordfhip of *Lough-*

A                                                                                        *borough*

There had been schemes to make the Soar route navigable from the River Trent to Loughborough as early as 1634. Thomas Skipwith had obtained powers to make a navigable waterway but it was not until the Act of 1776 that the project became a reality known as the Loughborough Navigation. This enabled 'cuts' and other necessary works to be carried out which in turn made the Soar accessible to barge traffic. The consequence of this was to reduce sharply the price of coal and other produce coming to Loughborough. For most of the 1780s the annual dividend paid to shareholders was over 100%. Such profits encouraged an Act of 1794 which enabled the canalization of the Soar to be extended to allow Leicester to share in the prosperity. (See p. 46 for tonnage figures).

The Boat Inn at Loughborough was one of the calling places for bargees who could obtain refreshments there for themselves and their horses. The bridge carrying Meadow Lane is the modern one which replaced the characteristic brick design adopted by the canal-builders in the 1790s. The works either side of the canal banks indicate the advantages that canals brought, for supplying raw materials and taking away some of the finished products.

The bridge over the canal at Loughborough carries the road to Nottingham. To the left stands the Commercial Hotel and behind it the large factory building where Morleys once made hosiery. It subsequently became a factory where pharmaceuticals were produced for the Riker Company, later The 3Ms Company. On the right John Jones's Foundry and Engineering Works flanks the canal.

In 1965 a dozen barges carrying timber from London to Nottingham were moored outside The Albion Inn in Loughborough for several days until the flooded River Trent had subsided. The total weight of the consignment was about 180 tons and the barges held about thirty men, women and children. Freight traffic by this time was rarely seen at Loughborough. When the canal was busy in earlier times The Albion provided food and lodging for bargees and their draught horses.

Coal was unloaded from barges at Loughborough by a steam shovel. In the background stands the tall building of the retort house erected in 1936 to increase production from the gasworks where coal was coked to produce town gas.

The canal basin at Loughborough in the 1960s is nearly deserted. However, its quays were once the scenes of much bustling activity. Industrial users of coal included the nearby gasworks, whose holders were removed in the early 1980s. Behind the building on the left lay the Loughborough Corporation Electricity Generating Station. It was built early in the twentieth century and continued in production until the national grid for electricity supplies made the Loughborough works redundant.

The lock-keeper's house at Loughborough in 1968. The house was erected when the canal was excavated in the late eighteenth century, although the windows give it a more modern appearance. Lock-keepers collected tolls from all users of the canal and operated the locks so as to minimize the loss of water from the canal. The income from tolls paid the wages of the keeper and costs of repairs, while the remainder was remitted to the company headquarters.

One of the recurrent problems for the commercial use of canals was caused by ice in cold weather. The icebreaker-barge is at work on the canal near Loughborough during a cold spell.

Pleasure-boats became more common on the canal near Loughborough between the two world wars. The growth of the leisure industry had its effects on the Soar as commercial activities were waning.

The lower Cotes Mill, beside the Soar at Loughborough, is now a restaurant, but until the mid-twentieth century it was a working water-mill. In its last years it specialized in producing animal feed and ceased production in 1958. The chimney indicates where the steam-engine augmented the available water power.

Corn ground at Cotes Mill was the subject of a major legal dispute in the seventeenth century. The Earl of Moira wanted to revive the ancient right of forcing all his tenants and the freeholders in Loughborough to use his mill instead of using the services of the cheapest mill in the district. The Loughborough case began in the reign of Charles I and continued until 1697 when the verdict went against the Earl.

Flooding at Cotes Mill remained a continual problem despite efforts to regulate water flows by flood elevation schemes.

A Swithland slate gravestone in All Saints churchyard, Loughborough, records the sad fate of Thomas Holt, who was killed by the wheel of the overmill at Cotes in 1767.

Nichol's *History of Leicestershire* illustrates the medieval bridge that carried the road from Nottingham and north-east Leicestershire across the Soar to Loughborough. Upkeep of the bridge was the responsibility of the Bridgemasters of Loughborough whose income came from rents of properties bequeathed by benefactors. These included Thomas Burton, a locally born wool merchant of the Staple at Calais in the fifteenth century. The bridge still survives but lies hidden beneath the accretions that enable it to carry modern traffic.

The bridge across the river at Stanford-on-Soar once carried the road from the village to Loughborough. Now it stands isolated because of the building of the Great Central Railway during the 1890s. This entailed diverting the course of the river and resiting the roadway. Nonetheless, users of the bridge paid a toll to the keeper, the last one of whom died in 1932. Two years later his house was demolished.

The viaduct over Loughborough meadows was built for the Great Central Railway and was photographed by S.W.A. Newton who recorded the whole of the construction of the last main line from Annesley to Marylebone (London). This viaduct was just one of the many major engineering feats necessary to complete the task. The existing road from Stanford to Loughborough had to be re-routed and a new course made for the River Soar. The method of building the nine arches involved using timber scaffolding to support high quality blue engineering brick. This gave the structure durability as well as an impressive appearance.

The completed railway viaduct of the Great Central Railway crosses the River Soar near Stanford. The line became fully operational for passenger services in 1899. It was intended to operate through services to Paris via the company's channel tunnel. This was never dug and the beautifully engineered line was not profitable. It ceased to carry traffic along its entire length after the Beeching Axe was wielded in 1963.

Inspecting the work in progress for the Great Central at Stanford-on-Soar in the mid-1890s was not only a matter for the specialists.

The meadow lands in the Soar Valley near Loughborough were crossed by streams that drained the river basin. To the top left is the village of Cotes. The Great Central Railway crosses the top right of the picture.

Limehurst Natural History Island was located in what was a loop of the River Soar near its junction with the canal, north of Loughborough. The river cut across the loop and left an island which was rather inaccessible. In 1952 Mr P.R.H. Dutton (Percy), a member of staff at Limehurst School, started the Limehurst Natural History Society. There were soon seventy youth members, many of whom helped to construct a wooden observatory on the island. In 1961 fire destroyed the hut. With the help of local donations of bricks, timber, money and with the aid of willing experts members built a new palatial observatory. The only access to the island for building materials and members was by the chain ferry as shown.

The new observatory, opened in 1963, contained a sunroof, laboratory, sleeping quarters, a galley, and a pool for aquatic specimens. Many local dignitaries extolled the project including Sir Robert Martin who said 'The society encouraged boys to take an interest in the natural world around them.' Today, unfortunately, the building does not exist except as a ruin, but the island is still known as Dutton's Island. It should be noted that the county boundary, which follows the course of the river, has changed so that the land inside the loop is now in Nottinghamshire.

# SECTION SIX

# The River becomes the County Boundary

Picnicking was a delightful way of enjoying the River Soar in summer-time before the First World War. The photographer, Mr Arthur Church Kirby, lived on his houseboat, *Mimosa*, moored by the bank.

The old and new forms of transport in 1912 were trapped by Soar floodwaters near Dishley. Motor cars were a sufficient novelty to attract the interest of the crowd.

Flooding at Hathern early in the twentieth century allowed children to enjoy the unusual experience of a ride along the road in a punt.

The old willows in flooded fields are between Hathern and Zouch early in the century. By tradition these used to be pollarded regularly by the river authorities or they would become top-heavy and split. There were mainly two varieties – the crack willow and the white willow.

A leisurely scene by a bend in the river near to Hathern shows how the riverside can be adapted for moorings.

The church of St James at Normanton-on-Soar stands in the background as the old chain ferry saves a long walk down to Zouch weir. For a small fee the ferryman or woman would haul the boat across by a chain that was permanently anchored to each side and ran along the river-bed. The only problem was how to attract the attention of the ferry operator.

A picnic in 1895 on the banks of the river at Normanton-on-Soar was a very civilized and gentle way of passing summer weekends. All but one of the group is a member of the Paget family.

These idyllic boating scenes reflect the simple joys of a bygone age. The lawn of The Plough Inn can be seen in the background below.

The landlords of The Plough Inn at Normanton-on-Soar doubled as coal merchants in the past and today's pretty lawn was yesterday's coal and stone wharf where barges unloaded.

Loughborough Boat Club Regatta. Loughborough Boat Club was formed in 1881 and for years boated from Barnsdall's wharf on Derby Road in Loughborough. After the Second World War the club had to move and its few boats were stored at one side of The Plough lawn at Normanton, also the scene of the annual regatta. In those days the regatta included sailing races and mop-fights as well as rowing races. The large crowd on the lawn is enjoying such a regatta early in the century.

The Manor House at Normanton-on-Soar is close by The Plough Inn. In the 1890s Mrs Rowland, the owner, threw open the grounds for the Loughborough and District Boat Club Regatta. Marquees were erected and Loughborough Borough Prize Band entertained. To add to the festivities Freddie Beck's excursion barge carried supporters from Loughborough with music provided by the Fifth Leicester Regiment. A bugle sounded five minutes before each race and the end of the races was marked by a pistol shot.

Before and after the Second World War the Loughborough Boat Club used farmland next to the Manor House grounds for its annual regatta. Temporary landing-stages were erected and marquees covered the field. Other boat clubs visited from near and far. These racing fours are approaching the finish having started up river near the ferry crossing. The Manor House wall is to the right.

A punt glides slowly past regatta spectators who have gathered on the tow-path at Normanton-on-Soar.

Normanton's regatta provided a good day out by the river bank. John Jones and Ernest Coltman (nearer the camera) were regatta patrons.

A number of small riverside bungalows were built between Normanton and Zouch near the beginning of the twentieth century and later. This was an earlier one owned by Mr Marshall Green, a well-known Loughborough tailor. It was a holiday retreat by the river. Note the floor raised above flood level, the verandah, landing-stage and the inevitable punt.

A horse and cart crosses the old Zouch Bridge. In front of it is the old foot-bridge over the weir.

Zouch canal bridge was constructed in 1778 to carry the turnpike road over the new canal. It was an arched cast-iron bridge and cost £20.

The cast-iron bridge at Zouch was removed in 1960 when there was a need to rebuild it to take the extra traffic load

A bridge across the Soar had existed at Zouch since Edward II's reign (1307–27) but it was a narrow stone pack-horse bridge only 2 yd wide and it fell into a state of disrepair. It was replaced by a new bridge nearby in 1793. In 1989 the medieval stone foundations were dredged out of the mud.

This three-arched bridge across the river at Zouch was built in 1793 at a point where there had been a ford. The cost of £700 was shared by Nottinghamshire and Leicestershire. It replaced the nearby pack-horse bridge.

The 1793 County Bridge was too narrow for twentieth-century traffic to pass. In 1930 a new bridge was constructed next to the old one. It was opened in 1931. The picture shows the newer bridge on the left while the old bridge is being demolished to the right.

Until recently the fields near Zouch had been subject to flooding whenever the river was high.

The road between Zouch and County Bridge was often flooded and a raised walkway was used earlier in the twentieth century. This bus struggles on the wrong side of the road to find a safe passage.

A father ferries his children in a punt down the road at Zouch in 1910.

A farmer has to rescue his sheep from floods at Zouch.

In recent years Severn Trent Water Authority spent much money deepening the middle miles of the River Soar by about 2 metres. This has allowed the river to take potential flood water away in greater quantity. The machine here is helping with this process.

The dredged materials are deposited well back from the river to create a new raised flood bank. These machines are involved in this operation.

There has been a mill at Zouch to grind corn since before 'Domesday Book' in 1086. In 1777 the Zouch 'cut' was constructed as part of the canalization of the Soar to Loughborough and in 1800 the Loughborough Navigation Company bought the mill for £1,000 so that it could better control the canal waters that the miller had diverted into the mill stream. By 1832 the firm of Paget and White leased the mill and operated as worsted-spinners and corn-millers. Worsted-spinning had ceased by 1861 and in 1863 a fire caused serious damage.

This is the tail of the mill-race at Zouch Mill. The old building has been converted into flats. In 1864 Samuel Goodacre rented the mill and enlarged it. Later, in 1870, he convert-ed it to a plaster mill to grind gypsum. The gypsum (in lump form) was brought from the Kingston-on-Soar mines by horse and dray, steam traction-engines and Sentinel lorries. Men hammered the large lumps into smaller pieces on the wharf and barrowed them into the mill to be crushed to a fine powder. This was then hauled in horse-drawn barges to Birmingham where it was used in the paper-making and plaster of paris industries. In the 1900s a petrol engine was brought in to help with the milling. By the 1920s gypsum grinding ceased.

Gypsum grinding ceased in 1925 and the mill reverted to grinding corn. At this time Edward Taylor bought the mill and outbuildings. He later owned most of Zouch. This is part of the old mill-wheel at Zouch that was being repaired in 1950. It had not been used since 1945. Mr Holden and Mr Axten are working on the conversion

This wooden building raised up on pillars stands next to Zouch Mill and was known as 'The Moulin Rouge'. People came from Loughborough and Belton at weekends to dance, eat and drink. Fishermen used the facility on Sundays. Timber, boats and other items were stored under the building.

Narrow lawns border the canal at Zouch. To the right is the old mill manager's house and the building to the left used to be part of the stables. Off the picture to the left is The Rose and Crown Inn which was called The Bull's Head until 1862 and provided accommodation for the bargees and stables for their horses.

The Zouch canal cut, built in 1777, joins the river in the foreground. Behind the lock in the distance is a foot-bridge constructed over the canal in 1787 to allow the continuation of the footpath from Hathern to Sutton Bonington. This footpath had led from the original pack-horse bridge that would have been to the right of the picture.

A haymaking scene on Tongue Island near to the Devil's Elbow of the Soar in 1914. The barge is travelling along a channel that was made in 1826 to improve the journey by avoiding so difficult a bend. The channel is called Jimmy Gadd's Cut after the contractor who made it

The aerial view of the Soar floods in the early 1970s shows that Sutton Bonington's location is just above flood level and helps to show why it is a long narrow village. It is possible in places to pick out the course of the river. The railway line had to be embanked for much of its route. Ratcliffe-on-Soar Power Station smokes and steams in the distance.

This road between Kegworth and Sutton Bonington passes close to Kingston-on-Soar and, with its raised foot-bridge, is reminiscent of the Barrow to Quorn road, which suffers the same problem with flooding.

The coot is typical of river life along the Soar. The bird life includes heron, snipe, woodcock, greater spotted woodpecker, pied and yellow wagtails, reed and sedge warblers, reed bunting, siskin, red poll and golden eye plovers, great crested grebe, waterfowl and Canada geese. Winter visitors include redwing, fieldfare, golden plover, and ducks such as widgeon, teal and shoveler, tufted, pochard and goldeneye.

When Loughborough Boat Club had to leave the Normanton stretch in the 1960s it moved its annual regatta to a longer and straighter course on the Sutton Bonington side of the river just above Kegworth. It was a good site although everything had to be set up during the two weeks before the event. In July 1973 there was a flood of over 3 ft of water across the regatta field and from that date the event moved to Nottingham's National Water Sports Centre. The floods had won.

This is an early picture of The White House Inn that stands by itself on the road between Loughborough and Kegworth. In the 1860s it was called The Navigation and had a wharf where barges unloaded coal, probably for nearby villages. It was here in 1953 that the Soar Boating Club was founded.

The Soar Boating Club was born in the lounge of The White House Inn in Kegworth in 1953, the year the first boat rally was held. Over the years various trophies such as the Arthur Warner Silver Tray for 'seamanship, leadership, and sportsmanship' have been presented. The first Whitsuntide cruise was to Burton-on-Trent in 1955. In the early days most club members' boats were of the 'Broads' design or were converted ships' lifeboats. In later years cruising narrow boats suitable for 7 ft locks were used. In 1961 the club purchased a river-side field at Normanton-on-Soar. Moorings were constructed, services laid on, a workshop hut was built and a slipway constructed. In 1972 the building of a clubhouse began. By 1978, 150 boat crews were members of the Club that still flourishes today. The picture below shows boats moored near to the weir at Zouch.

A quiet Sunday afternoon on the Soar in the Kegworth area during the Edwardian era.

The flood-lock at Kegworth is near to the main road bridge. It was built at the same time as the new canal stretch was cut in 1825 and is normally left open.

A row of spectators on the bridge at Kegworth watch as passengers board a large pleasure boat for a trip on the river. A gramophone at one end provided music for the afternoon entertainment.

Kegworth deep lock is shown with the church in the background. There was once a swing bridge nearby that enabled farmers to take corn over to the mill.

*Blue Moon* glides quietly along a placid River Soar. The canopy was a shelter from rain or sun.

Kegworth weir is shown here in full spate. It is crossed by a foot-bridge.

Kegworth deep lock is pictured around 1900 with Winser's Plasterboard Mill to the right. There had been a mill to grind corn since before the Domesday Survey of 1086. In 1790 the mill-wheel operated a trip mechanism to drive an iron forge supplied by cargoes of iron from Birmingham. The bump of the hammer was heard for miles. By 1812 this mill had reverted to grinding corn. In 1870 Winser and Co. bought an existing gypsum mine at Gotham and leased the Kegworth mill to grind gypsum. This was carried by horse and cart from Gotham, each load weighing a ton. The mill closed in 1904 and the site was then used for the peeling and preparation of osiers that were grown on the mill land and at Ratcliffe. The basket-making industry was based at the mill until around 1950. The building subsequently fell into disrepair and has since disappeared.

Kegworth Bridge has four arches in Nottinghamshire and one in Leicestershire. The original bridge was there in 1315 and a later one was built of stone and demolished in 1785. The new bridge, built of stone from Bunny Hall, was 195 ft long and 14 ft wide with five arches. Barges had difficulty in negotiating the bridge and many accidents occurred. A new cut was dug in 1825 to help solve the problem and an extra arch was built onto the bridge to span the canal.

William Pegg Woolley fished from his skiff early in the century at Kegworth. He appears to have been a skilful fisherman, judging by the size and amount of fish landed on the bank.

Flooded washland at Kegworth in the 1970s indicates the extent of the flood plain. Pylons overlook the scene.

A group enjoy the peaceful setting near Kegworth weir, and the quiet, simple pleasures of a picnic in the fresh air, away from the smoky factory chimneys of the towns.

# SECTION SEVEN

# Journey's End

One of the severest winters of the twentieth century occurred in the early months of 1947. Heavy snowfalls and deep frosts caused much suffering because food and fuel shortages still continued after the Second World War. When the thaw came in March extensive flooding along the Soar produced scenes like this one on a farm at Ratcliffe-on-Soar.

The Central Electricity Generating Board built the massive Ratcliffe-on-Soar Power Station during the 1960s, dwarfing the fourteenth-century parish church of Holy Trinity. Eight cooling towers 112.5 metres high use about sixty million litres of water drawn from the Soar daily. Power stations have to cool the steam to below 20° C before returning it as water to the river. A higher temperature would kill the fish. This was one of a series of major stations built along the Trent Valley during the 1950s and 1960s to meet the electricity needs of central England. Supplies of coal for the generating station came by merry-go-round freight trains running continuously from Midland mines. The Ratcliffe station produces about 2,000 megawatts, enough to supply the work and home needs of a population of one million people (about the size of Leicestershire).

The weigh-in for the Cobden Angling Society's fishing match took place at Ratcliffe on a Sunday morning in the 1940s.

Cobden Angling Society, *c.* 1946. The end-of-season match at Ratcliffe was a good opportunity to take a club photograph. The club was founded in Long Eaton over eighty years ago.

A fisherman at Ratcliffe catches a dace in the shallows, *c*. 1950. This natural shallow loop was the old course of the river now known as 'The Golden Mile' and was set aside for fishing. The Soar at that time contained plenty of chub, a few barbel, and grayling, but roach had largely disappeared. Anglers have been very aware of pollution and since the 1960s the authorities have succeeded in improving the quality of the waters.

Bank erosion at Ratcliffe-on-Soar was typical of many of the outside bends along the river. The river authorities have been making good such damage for years in order to prevent it spreading and in many places have built artificial banks of wood, concrete and steel.

This farm at Ratcliffe-on-Soar suffered in the floods of April 1947. The river at Ratcliffe has always been shallow and at one time could not comfortably take traffic. James Brindley, the canal engineer, suggested in 1766 that, instead of deepening the Soar, a bypass canal be built. In 1777 a cut-off canal was made to avoid the Ratcliffe shallows. Stepping-stones and fords were ways of crossing to Kegworth long ago.

Holiday-craft emerge from the Redhill Lock in 1977. These pylons branching out from Ratcliffe Power Station are not a pretty sight.

Redhill Lock is the last on the journey downhill to the Trent but the first on the journey towards Loughborough and Leicester.

This old scene of Redhill Lock and Bridge shows the small isolated community which, for the boatmen and their families of long ago, was a point of contact with the world at large. In the earliest days boats had to be hauled by windlass via a 'staunch' or flashlock at Redhill. James Brindley had the normal lock built later.

A pleasant walk by the river bank near Redhill marks the beginning of the end of the river's journey.

This engraving shows, to the right, the Soar entering the Trent at the end of its forty mile journey. The Redhill Tunnel, with its ornate entrance, was constructed in 1838–9 to allow through travel from Nottingham to Leicester by the Midland Counties Railway. Barge horses waited to do their stint on the tow-path. A system of ropes hauled the coal barges across the Trent from the Erewash side.

Where the Soar joins the Trent there was a need at times to ferry horses across the rivers from tow-path to tow-path.

# Acknowledgements

It is a pleasure to acknowledge the help of those who offered information and lent pictures for this publication. We have tried to find all owners of copyright and include them in this list. If there are omissions we will correct them in any later edition.

Brian Antrobus; Reg Baker (photographer); Michael Barker; M. Barnwell; Gordon Bignell; L. Eric Boon; A.W. Bourne; Revd Bro. Cave; Syd Cherry; G.A. Chinnery; Sheila Cooke; Tony Cox; Catherine Crawford; Dr David Crawford; Peter Davenport; Ann Devitt; Beryl M.Davies; Lesley Davis; Lynn Doylerush; J. Duffin; Steve England; A.R. Evans; John and Wendy Evans; Ronald Felstead; Mrs D.Firth; John Freeman; John Gagg; Peter Gamble; Nigel Garton; Harry Godfrey; Anthony Green; Colin Green; Mrs S. Greg; L. Hales; Revd L.Hancock; Mrs W. Haunton; Harry Haynes; Mrs M.A. Holman; R.A. Jamieson; R.P.Jarrett; Robin Jenkins; K. Jessup; Peter Jones ARPS; A.Kenney; Roger Lane; ChristopherLong; Dr John Martin; Dr J.F. Martin; John McNaughton; Brenda Moore; Ron Morris; William Moss; Dr Marilyn Palmer; Ruth Pointer; Miss E. Pulford; Dorothy Ritchie; Mrs E. Roberts; Ian Scott; J.C.S. Scott; Helen Shacklock; Jean Sims; John Slater; Barry Smith; Brian W. Smith; Mike Smith; Graham Spencer (Tarmac Ltd); Peter Spenlove-Spenlove; Aubrey Stevenson; H.W. Tempest; Don Thompson; Keith Thompson; Kevon Thompson; Jim Tomlinson; J.Towlson; A. Trehearne; R. Venner; T.M. Ll. Walters; Eric Webster; R. Weston; Mrs W. Whalton; Mrs S. Wileman; John Wilford; Ms P. Wilkinson; Brian C.J. Williams; M.J. Willis; Michael Wills; Mrs G.M. Wix; Eric Wright; Mrs J. York.

Aerofilms Ltd; T. Bailey Forman Ltd; Birstall and District Local History Society; Boat Museum; British Waterways; Cobden Angling Club; Croft Parochial Church Council; Garendon High School; Hathern History Society; *Hinckley Times;* John Doran Gas Museum; Kegworth Village Association; Leicester Rowing Club; Leicester Bishop Street Local History Library; *Leicester Mercury;* Leicestershire County Archives and Museums Service; Leicestershire County Library Service; Loughborough Boat Club; *Loughborough Echo*; National Rivers Authority; *Nottingham Evening Post*; Peter Le Marchant Trust; Powergen plc; RVB Photography (Whetstone); Severn Trent Water; Soar Boating Club; Sutton Bonington History Society.